HONEY & STONE

A collection of poems by

ALISON BARR

Printed by Firpress Printers, Workington.

Cover photo of Crummock Water and Mellbreak by the author.

To Mum, Dad, Nick and Alan.

Thank you for all of your help editing and proofing,
but most of all for believing in me.

CONTENTS

TELLING THE BEES   7
   Telling the Bees
   Polished Stones
   Castlerigg
   Diamond Ring
   Twilight Bird, Eaglesfield
   Queen of Flowers
   Mosedale Holly, Blencathra
   Out of Step, Out of Tune
   Tea with a Damselfly, Snowdrops

THE PRICE OF COAL   19
   Screen Lass
   Fairy Rock
   Pithead
   The Price of Coal
   Red Bricks and Blue Skies
   We are Clay
   Doorways
   A Magic Place, Wolf
   Keswick, Original Home of the Pencil Industry
   Rock Rainbows
   The Old Man

BEACHES AND BYWAYS   37
   Motorway
   The Tide Machine
   D-Day
   Welsh Malabar
   In the Interests of Dragons
   Wing Mirror Man

COKE GATHERERS   47

    Joseph Barr 1914
    Wild Ride
    1945
    Coke Gatherers
    Uncle John
    Carbon Copy
    The Optimism of Youth
    The Thorn and the Petal
    Council Flat Caramels
    Bird in a Stone
    Blackbird
    Recompense

DESTITUTION WALL   67

    No Man's Land, Corrour
    Saint Mary's Chapel, Grandtully
    Fillian
    Destitution Wall
    The Importance of Potatoes
    Nousts
    Ghost Bird
    The Philosophy of Eggs
    Invasion
    Aga
    Song of the Weaver
    Loom
    Star Man
    Zaragoza
    Snow Bride
    Otter, Blue Tit, Soloist,
    Autumn Ladies, The Writer
    Oriental Snow

HONEY AND STONE   95

    Honey and Stone
    Rotten Pigs and Wheat Seed
    Ammonite
    La Rochette
    La Dernière Cuillère

TELLING THE BEES

a skep full of honey ♦ arval ale and funeral cakes ♦ the corpse road ♦ polished stones

hefts and Herdwicks ♦ Castlerigg stone circle ♦ penumbral shadows ♦ twilight bird

Queen of flowers ♦ Mosedale holly ♦ Blencathra ♦ snowbonnets ♦ tea with a damselfly

TELLING THE BEES

He wears his Sunday best,
she a simple dress.
A gift of wedding cake
is left by the skeps,
petal-decorated.

They dance the dance of love,
bees dance the dance of flowers.

The couple set up home.
Skeps are placed in bee boles
in the south facing orchard wall.
New queens and swarms
lay claim to plaited domes.

Wax comb cells, nectar-crammed,
are fanned, transformed, capped.

A cradle is carved
to hold their son.
They tap tap the hive
with the house key
to announce his birth.

Yellow catkins, pollen loaded,
dust the swarm, honey flows.

Years pass, she passes,
it is time to talk to the bees.
Black mourning cloths
are draped over skeps.

White-cloaked hawthorns
hunched twilight ghosts.

The old man summons his son.
"When I am gone you must
tell the bees, if not they will die
and there'll be no more honey."

Mist shrouds the corpse road
from Loweswater to Saint Bees.

His son visits the hive,
tells them that father has gone.
They are the first to know.
Ice, wind, snow. Bees
murmur through stone walls.

Two guests from each farmstead
are bidden to honour Ambrose.

Hives are lifted,
carefully put back down.
The beekeeper's coffin
is lowered into the earth.
Arval ale and biscuits are offered.

Frozen silence of the grave,
warm stillness of the hive.

POLISHED STONES

Erratic boulders rest on bleak moors.
Rough conglomerate, glacial grooved,
weather scarred. Girths and undersides
smoothed by the rubbing of sheep.

Sunken hollow, sweet smell of droppings.
Herdwicks have pawed here for generations,
sharp hooved, Lakes-bred, sheltering
from storms, scorching sun, blizzards.

The heft provides a treasured sleeping spot,
a place to lie side by side with new lambs.
Stones shine, lanolin glossed, fleece snagged,
balanced on peat pedestals.

CASTLERIGG

A stone circle
furred with frost
stolen from a white hare.

Mountain ringed.
Skiddaw, Blencathra,
Helvellyn, Grasmoor.

Naddle Beck teases
silver meltwater,
Solway destined.

Wind wraiths chase
down cold dales.
Sleet veils the Carles.

Over millennia,
sun, moon, stars,
arc across thin horizons.

DIAMOND RING

Distant flares erupt,
white hot.

Mist curls and wisps
above Loweswater.

Light slips from
the heron's back.

Clouds, sedge, water,
fade to pewter.

Three spheres align,
Terra, Luna, Sol.

I fit my finger
into the ring of light.

TWILIGHT BIRD,
EAGLESFIELD

A white owl whooshes
towards the front of my car;
wings wide as the windscreen,
face round as a headlamp,
lit up, staring in at me.

"I am not an angel,
I am the voice inside you.
Soft snow dusting winter fells,
a span of feathers from long ago."

He ghosts in cold air.
My car crunches
sparkling ice glass.
The hedgerow channel
is furred, frost laden.

"I am not an angel,
I am the story inside you.
Look and you will find me,
a cross of silver from long ago."

The red digital display reads
minus three, the heater is on max.
I stop the car, turn off the engine,
stand in silent twilight.
Large feathers begin to fall.

QUEEN OF FLOWERS

They say that when she was born
the room became a garden
and blood spots on the sheets
became a scatter of red petals.

Her mother was the Queen of Flowers.
She took the new babe
in her arms, wrapped in a shawl
woven from yellow-eyed daisies
and nursed her with sweet nectar milk.

The child grew to have lily smooth skin,
golden hair that flowed like honey
and smelled of honeysuckle.
She spoke only the language of flowers.

Everyone was charmed by her,
perceived in her their flower preferred.
Nocturnal jasmine, yellow silks.
Fragrant lavender, lilac linen.
Heady rose, crimson satin.

As the sun swept low in a darkened sky,
she dressed in furs and snowdrop boots.
All who loved her offered sprigs of holly,
pungent ivy, soft pansies and cyclamen
which she pinned in her frosted hair.

She married the King of Winter,
he of ice and storms,
who made living things dormant.
Come spring, they sat on a high fell
and sang a song of seasons.

She scattered perfumed blossoms
and whispered to sleeping bees.
He lifted a corner of frost
and pulled it from the cold land.

MOSEDALE HOLLY

Solitary,
rooted into shale

below Mellbreak's flanks.

Knarled limbs,

grey lichen mottled,

hold up the waxen leaf dome.

Around her,

moor flowers, Herdwicks, bracken.

The silver beck, a constant companion.

BLENCATHRA

pulls itself out of the valley
up from the bracken
into the long summit

that sits under
a sky arch canopy
pale silk blue.

OUT OF STEP, OUT OF TUNE

I am a walking Aeolian harp.
Wind whistles through my crutches,
droning eerily through height holes.
My silver flute sticks prop me up
and entertain me, as I attempt
the short circuit, yet again.
Crutches forward, bend bad leg, keep
heel down, step through with good leg.
Sometimes we are almost in time,
step, drone, step, drone, step, whistle,

The black cat from the farmyard
sneaks out to greet me, rubs longingly
against my leg. The wind blows,
my false leg lets out a high pitched whine.
Mr Lucky Black turns tail
and goes scooting off down the road.
Pensioners from the village overtake me
with glee. Thank goodness old Minshaw's
memorial bench is coming into sight.

Primroses are more yellow,
the habits of birds more familiar.
Maybe harmony will come in time.
For the moment I am a four-legged,
propped up half ghost, wailing tunes
of annoyance.

TEA WITH A DAMSELFLY

At Lodore Falls Hotel
a damselfly alights on my table.

Head compass pointing
into the breeze,

betrayed
only by a quiver of wing.

A teaspoon,
long and silver.

I sip my Earl Grey,
transfixed.

It takes off in a blur.
A mini feat of engineering.

SNOWDROPS

You alight from the carriage of spring,
step daintily into winter wastelands,
gather in crowds under hedgerows.
Pure white bonnets hide delicate faces.

THE PRICE OF COAL

Haig Pit ♦ screen lass ♦ slate and stone ♦ pithead ♦ Fairy Rock ♦ Margaret Ann

red bricks and blue skies ♦ Solway clay ♦ border walls ♦ Harrington doorsteps

steel ♦ magnesite ♦ graphite ♦ haematite rainbows ♦ mines and quarries ♦ atoms

SCREEN LASS

1

She hurries up to High Kells,
white skirts billowing.

Saltom cliffs are a red drape,
hemmed with dark seaweed,
tugged by the tide.

The horizon as thin
as a tern's wing.

She climbs down into shadows
of sea-salt and sandstone
and begins to carve.

Her initials curve
in loops of bird flight,

next to a fossil
locked in stone.

11
Now bent to her job,
she picks out slate and stone
from the coal.

After the long shift at Haig Pit
she flies along the coastal path,

runs her finger
around the smooth grooves
of her name;

bright, red, eternal.

FAIRY ROCK

Meteorite black, scorched.

This rock has a lure,
an 'asking to be written on',
silent beckoning.

A man takes out a knife
and carves his initials.
Others follow.

It becomes a monument
to the workers of Whitehaven.

Winds whip up storms
that hammer the coast.

The rock shifts,
water curls and hisses.

Typeset highlights.
Icy fingers claw
at foundations.

The Solway lifts it
and carries it into the sea.

Names of generations vanish.

*No-one could visit the Fairy Rock from any part of the world
without finding the initials of his name among the hundreds
that cover its surface.*   Joseph Wear

PITHEAD

Wheels lowered miners
into dank earth,

heaved up tubs of coal
into blinding daylight.

Long terraces of mining houses
hold memories of pit workers.

Those who came home,
those who didn't.

THE PRICE OF COAL

The deceased was SKELLY,
Margaret Ann, died 1906, aged 17.
Screener, Whitehaven Colliery Co. Ltd.

Last night they'd laughed
and spun and danced.
Margaret's flame of hair
shone out across the hall.

Another day, another shift,
shovelling coals onto the screens.
Waste gathers in dark tides
around their feet.

Revolving belts catch her skirt,
dragging her into the shafts.
Mary-Jane grabs her friend's hand
and screams for the overman.

The engine clatters to a stop.
They free Margaret from the machinery.
Her headscarf is ripped from her head,
auburn hair spills into black dust.

She was at once removed to the Infirmary,
where she died at twenty minutes past two
on Friday morning.

RED BRICKS AND BLUE SKIES

Up to their ankles in tides of red;
red dust, red clay, red bloom of effort.
My granddad and his father before him
worked at Whitehaven Brickworks.

Only Sundays could break the wall,
with a promise of fresh Solway air,
infinite blue skies and a small silver fish
caught down by the harbour on a thin line.

On Monday mornings they dragged
themselves to the temple of tall chimneys.
Grey smoke belched and gathered
above a town rendered into servitude.

Rumbling wagons tipped out rocks
to be shovelled into crusher jaws.
Millhouse wheels clattered,
screeched, ground, pressed.

Clay *pudding* churned in pugmills.
Hands threw clots into moulds
and packed sand-lined boxes.
Row after row, dark blood moist.

Men stacked brick upon brick
in long drying tunnels.
Air choked, powder penetrated.
Bricks *smiled* under pressure.

Fuel crackled and burned,
vast kilns throbbed heat.
Air drifted around chambers
like a high priest ghost.

The walls of their labour rose up
around them; homes, factories,
churches, viaducts, pit buildings,
lavish Georgian houses.

Frog marks echo people and places;
Kirkhouse, Sandysike, Micklam,
Harrington, Whitehaven, Camerton,
Barrow, Romans at Brampton.

Four sided cradles and coffins
bolstered the life in-between,
decreed extrusion of the soul.
The only relief, a blue sky Sunday.

Frog marks: These are indents in the top of the brick to be filled with mortar in order to maximise strength.
Smile: A distinctive crease (smile) which appears in bricks stacked for drying and put under pressure.
Pudding: A mixture of clay, sand and ash.

WE ARE CLAY

Timeworn towers speak across millennia
from Cumbria to Mesopotamia.
Hands scooped clay by Solway reed beds
and dug between the Tigris and Euphrates.
The Tower of Babel searched high for God.
By now He may have regretted forming
the shape of man in the Garden of Eden.

At the Empire's edge, Hadrian's Wall
and the river Eden, *Itouna* of rushing water,
yielded to a silver sea expanse.
Craftsmen pressed stamps into wet tiles,
preserving legions, emperors, the Empire.
Waxen masks peeled from the dead
stared blankly from wall niches.

Come let us make bricks and bake
them thoroughly. King James Bible.
Shape, stack, dry, kiln, fire, build.
Clay mingles with cobalt and sand.
Classic colours; Cumbrian Red, Fletton,
Staffordshire Blues, Accrington Bloods,
Silver Oxfordshire, London Browns.

Crumbling, powdery, smoothed, flecked.
Crevices are crammed with particles;
root, mineral, animal, shell, fish, petals.
Carboniferous atoms interconnect.
Sediment crushed, weathered, layered.
Water gushes over mountains, eroding
feldspar, *mother of clay*.

Existence over, men are laid to rest
under a thin skin earth, equal with the clay.
Castles and churches, rise, fall, crumble.
Border lines and walls shift with dark tides;
Hadrian's, Berlin, Jericho, Troy. And more.
Walls designed by minds echo barriers within.

DOORWAYS

Dad and I wander over uneven grass
in the middle of what was.
On the foreshore, bulldozed bricks,
mortar-crusted, speak generations.
Some with beginnings, some with endings,
one intact, which we place to the side.

Searching eroded banks, I uncover
blue and white crockery fragments,
wiring, a cup handle, lumps of coal,
a grimy ribbon, green bottle-glass.
Lifetimes and intimacy exposed,
home to sandpipers and sea daisies.

An old doorstep is laid out
at my feet like a gravestone.
A rusty handle catches my eye,
I pull the crumbling iron free,
feel the weight of a door
opening and closing.

It was here by the sandstone harbour,

between the Solway and the west coast line,

that 27 Henry Street once stood.

The birthplace of my grandfather,

a two-up two-down terrace,

in Harrington, factory black.

A MAGIC PLACE

Billy said that if you kick
at slag stones on Harrington beach
they split open and shine like polished mirrors,
so bright you can see your reflection.

Kevin said that when the steelworks
was still going, clouds of red dust
filled the air and birds flocked
from all around to soar on hot thermals.
White seagulls turned into pink flamingos.

Rita remembers two giant magnesite tanks
down by the harbour, circular ponds,
milky turquoise, magic swimming pools
where kids leapt and splashed like tropical fish.

And Jim, Jim told me about wrapping pasche eggs
in string, gorse petals, onion skins and newspaper
and boiling them in the pot over the range
until they were shiny red, hurrying
up to Milking Hill to roll, dump and eat them.

Janet's father worked a harbour Dredger,
each boat had a different coloured funnel.
They were named after gems:
Pyrope, Agate, Beryl, Girasol.
And the breakwater was all lit up
by a line of oil lamps with red lights.

Gala days were a favourite for all.
Especially the greasy pole,
when folks hit one another with pillows,
and the air filled with laughter and feathers.
In Harrington, a magic place.

WOLF

Dreamy
Istanbul
of the coast
sea spray
hazed
minaret
decorated
dome
glittered
beautiful

Sellafield.

KESWICK – ORIGINAL HOME OF THE PENCIL INDUSTRY

I select a black 12 and outline Catbells,
the lake, trees and clouds.
Derwentwater is shaded with blue 2.
Yellow 6 brings gorse to life.

At the invitation of the Virgin Queen,
German miners searched the hills for graphite.
Precious enough to warrant an escort to London.
Not for artists I hear you say. No, nothing as tranquil.
For cannonball moulds, shot and gun carriage lubricant.
The men of all things earthly and valuable lived in camps
strung along the lake shore and on the islands.
The place of The Whore's Hut, Portinscale,
bustled with sixteenth century comings and goings.

I choose green 4 sketching in the islands.
Brown 8 fills grassy hillsides.
I finish my sketch and place
the pencils into their metal box-tray.

Lakeland BY CUMBERLAND. COLOUR PENCILS.
ASSORTMENT FOR SCHOOL AND GENERAL USE.

ROCK
RAINBOWS

Sale Fell
Old mine
Workings
Expose
Solid
Slate wave
Curve
Oily rainbows
Locked
In stone
Brilliant
Iridescent,
Surface
Feathered
Dragged
By a handful
Of pastels,
Fluid
Shifting
Sunlit
Haematite
Rainbows
Elusive
In solids.

803 THE OLD MAN

Ground transforms to paper,
white, crisp, flat, smooth.
I walk past star-marked cairns,
old pits, stone circles.

Numbers increase 244, 381, 518,
803 OLD MAN OF CONISTON
black capital announced.
I stand in a blue dot triangle.

Red dotted lines guide me
over Brim Fell and Swirl How.
Two blue circles, Levers Tarn
and Low Water, stare up.

Double black lines indicate
Coppermine's valley path.
Mines (dis) Quarries (dis)
Church Beck rushes downhill.

Precision landscape,
Elegant cartography.
Numbers, symbols, colours,
names, contours, coordinates.

BEACHES AND BYWAYS

motorways and hard shoulders ♦ celestial bodies ♦ Normandy beachhead ♦ bullets

smooth grey slate ♦ dragons with metal scales ♦ Snowdon summit ♦ mirrors and gwals

MOTORWAY

Queues likely.
No hard shoulder for 300 yards.
No street lighting, Midnight to 5 a.m.
Keep apart 2 chevrons.
Check your distance.
Tiredness can kill. Take a break, 2 miles.
Police speed check area.

The Big Green Parcel Machine.
Asda saving you money every day.
Billington Fuels. Hazardous Substances.
Norfolk Line. Morspan Construction.
BP Tunderman. Wiseman Dairies.
Eddie Stobart. Norbert Dentressangle.
O'Reilly Transport. McBurney.
Pallet Line Shipping Ltd.
Bringing your home to life.

Animal Feed for a better future.
Goggins Transport. Galway.
Laura Ashley, Paris, London, NY.
Love bread. Love Kingsmills.
Scoraig, Inverness, Morecambe,
Folkestone, Dover, old Peugeot 406.
We take turns at driving.

Logistics, deliveries, express courier,
haulage, shipping, streamlined to save fuel.
Temperature controlled distribution.
Flammable Liquid. Excellence simply.
Supplying renewable energy.
Propel Yourself into the Future.

Recovery area. Await rescue.
Wide vehicles straddling.
River Ribble. Wigan Pier. A5209.
Blackpool Tower World. M55 Jn 32.
M6 The South. A426 Lutterworth.
Flyovers, barriers, Scania, F, D, P, NL, ES,
shredded tyres, sidings with long grass,
cans, wrappers and dirty tissues.
Costa, Burger King, Services 22km.
Food services. Feel the difference.
Bringing you the perfect lifestyle.

THE TIDE MACHINE

He grasps the polished handle
and begins to wind.

Harnessed pulley weights
rise and drop.
Wheels follow
the turning of the stars.

Brass components hold memories
of signals and sextants.

Moon-white paper,
stretched around cylinders,
rotates slowly.

A black pen creates curves
of time, sun, planets.

Astronomy,
gravity, trigonometry.
$F \text{ (tide)} = G \text{ (gravity) } M s / r^3$.

Tides translate,
ink wet, line-mapped.

The crank ceases.
He unravels charts
and analyses data.

The ebb and flow of seas
across the world is predicted.

Almanac booklets are dispatched to ports.
Ships sail, depending on the tides.

D-DAY

The chatter of young ladies can be heard.
They wear smart blouses and buttoned cardigans
pinned at the neck with glass brooches.
Men have done their clever job, of equations,
calculations and construction.
Many of them have joined the war now.

Thomas Doodson receives a 'MOST URGENT'
request from the Admiralty for precise tidal charts
for the landings on the beaches.
The ebb and flow lies in feminine hands.
Wheels of destiny began to turn,
mechanical imitation of gravity and orbits.

Small boats and midget submarines
carry out reconnaissance of Normandy beaches.
Predictions are linked to moonrise, moonset,
sunrise, sunset, twilight. Waves of men
are bound to the cosmos, and the ladies.

On the 6th of June 1944 the landings start.
The machines cannot measure the number of bullets
that thrash the water, the volume of blood
that mingles with the tide. Cannot foretell
the casualties at Omaha.

The ladies huddle around the radio
to listen to the BBC report on D-Day
from a Normandy beachhead:

The paratroops are landing
...they're landing all round me as I speak
...they've come in from the sea and they're fluttering down.
...and they're just about the best thing that we've seen
for a good many hours. They're showering in
...there's no other word for it.

German casualties on D-Day were around 1,000 men.
Allied casualties were at least 10,000, with 4,414 dead.

WELSH MALABAR

This coffee has been monsooned.
A new verb, meaning rain-soused,
washed to pale gold, bleached
by steamy monsoon storms.

Aberystwyth too is pale as a faded bean,
smooth grey slate, Irish Sea polished.
Shell white guesthouses stare
on to crema-froth beaches.

Sacks of Arabica travel the oceans,
from the lush forests of Karnataka
and Kerala, to The Mecca,
'Quality Tea and Coffee Merchant.'

Roasted beans patter onto silver scales.
The grinder crushes, releasing aromas
of chocolate and spice. Seaside town
rain drizzles down the window pane.

IN THE INTERESTS OF DRAGONS

– Please do not touch the dragon.
– Do not climb on the dragon.
– Do not fly on the dragon.

Gleaming dragons pop up everywhere.
Blue, red, copper, big as trucks.
Wings folded, wings outstretched.
Spike and claw festooned, metal-scaled.
Poised on lawn-ringed pedestals
decorated with slate chips and plants.
Empty eyes stare. Gaping jaws
breathe invisible fire.

– Do not put your hand into a dragon's mouth.
– Do not meet its eye for too long.
– Never speak to dragons.

Little pink-clad princesses
are fearful of dragons. Aren't they?
At the entrance to the campsite
is the most beautiful dragon of all.
I jump onto the big red's back
and kick its flanks. Long white ribbons
stream from my storybook coronet.

We circle Harlech castle, sweep golden beaches,
sit on Snowdon summit eating vanilla ice-cream
and watch over the land of Cymru.

WING MIRROR MAN

He roves the roads of Conway,
lantern light seeking tell-tale glints.

Passing cars illuminate
a figure in a long coat,
who merges into verge gwals.
A wizard, shadow,
or trick of the eye.
Glassy shards
in shattered slate
reflect his other selves.
Flat faced, locked in silver.
Collecting is his raison d'être,
winding roads his hunting ground.
Narrow bridges, tight bends,
intruding walls and rock faces
are where he gleans most.
Mercury bright, intact,
on stalks, fragmented mosaic,
fine-lined as spider webs.

Dazzling dragonfly wings repaired,
he goes darting down the Cymric valleys.

COKE GATHERERS

a tale of two cities ♦ silver and sweethearts ♦ mud filled trenches ♦ petals in ash

coke wagons ♦ steel and Stetsons ♦ carbon and chalk dust ♦ spiky bushes

parapets and lintels ♦ winter cathedral ♦ harling versus peat ♦ a bird on the tarmac

JOSEPH BARR 1914. WRITTEN BY ALISON BARR 2014

Thinned, scratched, dulled, battered, this dog tag has found its way back from an Ypres trench to a Coatbridge street, J BARR PTE 7134 HLI REG E. This and a beautiful Sweetheart brooch are all that she has now. Two silver circles, one of love, one of death. Some months before she had held a Celtic pin brooch in her hand. It was from a Glasgow jeweller, an expensive parting gift, a love token. She knows that he will not return. She rushes to the front door in her slippers, tears falling, shaking with shock, cold, empty like the street, holding only the ghost of his back.

He couldn't bear a fuss, not even a goodbye cuddle or kiss, typical Scot, didn't tell her, as an ex regular and reservist he packed his kitbag, put on his Glengarry, angled in defiance, and walked out of the door. He knows that he will not return to this house, his wife, his weans. He had told his sister, *"The only way I'll be returning is in a corned beef tin."* He does not look back. 2nd HLI men march to Motherwell rail station.

Within a week of arriving in France Joseph had fought in the battle of Marne alongside the French, who famously hired the Paris taxis to bring a reserve battalion to the fight. Paris was saved. The Germans were pushed to positions north of the river Aisne, where they dug in, establishing the lines for four years of trench warfare. 2nd HLI dug in to defend the strategic town of Ypres.

'We have been having a very hard time of it lately.'

After being shelled all day, on 7th November, the enemy attacked at 4 a.m. Jimmy from Kilmarnock shouted the alarm. The enemy were upon them. The HLI couldn't see well in the mist, 'only had time to fire a few rounds.' Figures jerked and loomed like shadow puppets. The Germans were in their trench, where only moments ago the watch had passed round smokes and hot tea. This was it then, hand to hand, eye to eye, man to man, shouting, bayonets, knives, kill or be killed, mud, tearing, slipping in filth, screaming, stabbing, everything too close; stubble on faces, a blue enamel mug lying on its side, veins throbbing at temples, smell of unfamiliar sweat, buttons and badges glinting, larger than life blades, prayers to mothers and loved ones, final gasps.

Lieutenant C.L. Cornish HLI, letter dated 10th of November. Killed on 11th of November, 1914.

'Three days ago when we were in the trenches the Germans attacked one of our Companies at four in the morning. They charged suddenly out of thick mist, and our men had only time to fire a few rounds before they were in the trench. A hand-to-hand fight ensued. The trench was a perfect shambles. I was in a trench to the left of all this and could hear a fearful din going on.'

The battle moved on. Joseph and seven of his comrades were buried by the Germans, alongside the German dead, in their cemetery at In de Ster, named after an inn used by German troops, The Star Inn.

In April 1915 two officers, one British, one German, met in no man's land and quietly exchanged a handful of dog tags. Wives and sweethearts will now know that their men are dead, after months of being listed as *'missing in action'*.

She fingers the dog tag in her hands, reads the letter, *'Killed in action, France and Flanders, 7th of November 1914.'* Why couldn't he have given her a last cuddle and kiss, instead of rushing away without saying goodbye? She knows why. None of it matters now anyway.

He departed, she got a brooch. He 'returned', she got a dog tag. She wraps them up in her best lace hankie and carefully places them in the bottom corner of the drawer. She goes downstairs to tell the weans, *"Yer Daddy's no' comin' hame. He was hurt in the war fightin' the Germans. He did it for us and he was very brave. We'll just be on our own frae' noo on. He's no' comin' back ever."*

Esther ties her apron strings and peels the tatties ready for dinner.

This is the story of my great-granddad Barr, written using factual military documents and family accounts. People said that he was the first man from Coatbridge killed and his name is recorded on the war memorial at Glenboig.

THE WILD RIDE

It's comin'. It's comin'.
Skinny legged kids
in school jackets
flock like a clutch
of excited sandpipers.

Silver rails and wires
hum to crescendo.
The round-eyed bug,
all madder and white,
clatters to a halt.

They scoot upstairs.
The motorman turns
his controller handle clockwise.
On the coast side,
shore and blue sky emulsion.

Newhaven lighthouse
gives them a thumbs up.
They glide past Starbank Park
and the Old Chain steamer pier.
Approach the S bend.

The tram veers left
then swings over to the right
balancing on the track edge.
She hangs out over the sea
like a tall Forth yacht.

And just for that instant
they are suspended
over water and dreams,
before she sashays down
to Granton Square Terminus.

1945

Joe wanders in from the street
and it startles him like a warning light.
A red petalled geranium beams
from the middle of the mantelpiece.
A bolt of colour exposing threadbare
poverty. His mother, in a mane of curlers,
says *"Your dad's coming home tomorrow."*

Daddy, daddy, daddy's coming home.
Dad, away for years, in a far off place,
a name at the end of a crumpled letter.
Joe trawls his memories. Drags up a man
in an overcoat who took him to the docks
and told stories about boxing in Coatbridge.
It would be good to have him home. Wouldn't it?

Tomorrow comes and with it daddy.
Four kids line up with comb-pulled hair
and pink scrubbed faces, excited, uncertain.
Jean gives him a cuddle. He looks at them.
"Hello dad." they say and stare. Joe wants
to ask what the war was like, but doesn't.
That evening they sit down to a special meal.

Dad slumps into mum's armchair,
puts on his old slippers and lights a cigarette.
Unfamiliar smoke and man smell fills the room.
The geranium screams out its welcome.
Within a week petals have fallen like blood
into spent fire ashes and dad has taken
to the spare room and the drink.

COKE GATHERERS

The hoose wis freezin' an' it a' started
with me an' ma wee sister Jean.
Faither led us o'er the wall intae the yard
an' showed us where the coke piles were.

Ye jist look normal, like yiz are oot fer a walk
an' ye jist pit a few bits in 'til yer bags are fu'.
Dinnae worry, everybody's daen it.
Yese'll no get intae trouble frae the 'thorities.

Aifter school we trauchled doon tae the shore road,
wi' oor gas mask schoolbags, collecting coke
by the satchelful. The place smelt o'diesel,
timber, sulphur. Holding tanks loomed above us.

If it wis cauld, oor hands went blue
an' oor skin peeled aff as we pulled lumps
oot o' the frozen heap. Wee Jean wisnae happy,
didnae want to go pickin' coke, but we'd been telt.

When we got hame we'd tip oot the bags
ontae the flair in front o' the fire.
The guid thing wis that it burnt hot as the devil,
so hot it burnt the erse oot o' the fire basket.

Efter a while Jean widnae dae it any mair
so me an' ma faither became partners in crime.
Him flingin' big chunks aff the wagons, me
packin' it in bags an' him fillin' up his 'coal coat'.

The two o' us staggered oot, weighed doon,
Dad lumpy, both o' us, hands black.
A young polisman stopped us once and said
"Ye've been gatherin' sea coal?" "Aye."

UNCLE JOHN

Studded boots chink on metal stairs,
one step after another, in constant rhythm.
At the top, by the railing, John pauses,
gazes at orange lights around the Clyde,
first slit of pink sun glinting to the East.

Door closed, he hangs up his bunnet
and takes the metal piece box
out of his World War One satchel.
He spoons tea and sugar
into a chipped enamel mug.
Steam curls rise in cold air.

All day, one hundred feet above the earth,
he waits for jobs to start,
reads westerns to while away the time.
Up in the cab, showdowns take place,
gun fights over ringletted, busty molls.
Saloon doors blim-blam back and forth,
stetsoned cowboys join him for tea breaks.

When cargo loading starts John moves levers,
handles shaped to his hands, responsive.
He becomes the *Man of the West,*
high on his leather saddle, lasso held tight.
The crane judders, luffs, rumbles,
hook dangling over docklands.

At sixty, with forty years service,
he trudges to work as usual with no special plan.
In the afternoon he climbs down from the cab,
walks away and daunders home, leaving a copy
of *Big Sky* and *True Grit* on the worn vinyl seat.
"Yer early", says his sister, *"Aye"* says John.

CARBON COPY

At the Craig and Rose paint factory,
mum pulls in her chair and begins to type.
Letters to architects, specifications, invoices,
keys rattle and hammer on the ink ribbon.
Fingers fly across the a to z, dotting full stops
that end, but do not end the sentence.
Carriages ting at the end of every line,
demanding to go back to the beginning.
And like red oxide Forth Bridge paint
the next day she goes in and starts again.

Dad folds up his shirt collar, tightens
the knot of his tie, does up his top button.
In Ferranti he pens figures into columns,
rounds up, rounds down, credit, debit,
pound signs, decimal points, calculators.
When the hardback bible is complete
it disappears into the great filing box
of financial machination and Dad comes
home stiff and tense as a faded ruler
that ends abruptly at thirty centimetres.

Andy, my brother, is an apprentice

at Letts diaries, Dalkeith. Every day

he trails across the road and waits

in the smoky bus shelter at the roundabout.

The machine thunders, spits, jams.

Adhesive weighs the air, binding people and pages.

Endless stacks pile up, to trim, fold, laminate.

In the evening he skulks home, slouches

on the sofa, eyes glazed. He told me once

that it was a war between him and the beast.

He hasn't talked about it since.

I dig my living with chalk,

carve trails and dates across blackboards

from Monday to Friday. Dust sticks to me

like funeral ashes and steals my soul.

Decades of spelling lists ebb and flow

with tides of children who sit at wooden desks

staring up at me from open jotters.

The square of light in the wall

a cheerless reminder of sun and hillsides.

THE OPTIMISM OF YOUTH

She sits in the reference room,
high domed, lined with books.
Silent, except for the turn
of a page, a reader's breath,
the laying down of spectacles
on a brown wooden desk.

I gather up papers,
buckle my leather satchel,
step into an empty street
that hides its grime
under layers of white.

Flakes swirl and dance.
Crossing the road she waits
for a number twenty-seven bus
that will never come. Waits
in this magical moment,
silver from head to toe.

I stand in a winter cathedral
filled with flight of owl,
feather vaulted, wing swept.
Lead lined windows
spill light down long aisles.

Soft fur drapes parapets
and lintels. Movement
ghosts over pavements,
faded footstep tracery.
Star webs hang on lashes,
stick to her hair and coat.

Powder flurries glitter and sparkle.
The city is mine. I take pleasure
walking in the middle of the road.
Go peacefully towards the altar
of unpolluted nothingness.

THE THORN AND THE PETAL

Dad would get up early to walk
five miles down Dalkeith Road to his office.
He'd take joy in flowers and bird song,
share with us, "*The blackthorn has flowered.*"

Now, as I cycle down the old Brigham road,
I pass dark spiky bushes that have burst
into creamy blossom under a spring sun,
waves of softness masking thorns.

Life too has beauty and harshness.
Dad is an old man in a poky council flat.
That evening I phone him to say
"The blackthorn is out."

COUNCIL FLAT CARAMELS

Dad sucks caramels,
contemplates the seasons
from his comfortable leather chair.

He looks out of a top flat window,
into the square.

Mind wanders over rooftops
beyond the Ness
beyond the years
to purple crowned Wyvis.

He is walking through heather.
Dad chews caramels.

BIRD IN A STONE

My lover picked up a beach pebble
and took out his pen.
He drew a black ink dove
with outstretched wings,
wrote *'A bird in a stone'*
and announced that it was me.

I pondered, what did it mean?
That I hadn't reached my potential?
That I wouldn't let go?
Had circumstance trapped me?
I didn't ask, went home, put the stone
in the bay leaf pot to stop the cats digging.

Two decades have passed, flown,
stone long gone. Image and words
still imprinted into my brain,
which has become the stone.
I carry it with me like an albatross
around my neck and must never look back.

I wish he'd never given me the bloody stone.
I really didn't want to know.
This bird has flown.

BLACKBIRD

Feathers merge with tarmac.
The bird is a flat black cross.

Wings outstretched
in static flight.

A glinting eye, still moist,
stares up at me.

The yellow beak open
in a last silent cry.

It is an origami template.
I fold it together.

Pull the tail
to make its wings beat.

RECOMPENSE

Unlike Seamus Heaney I do not earn
my living through the digging of a pen.
My parents were nothing as romantic as farmers,
did not come from a poetic place of machair,
orchids and peatlands.

We lived in a housing scheme,
all dog piss, concrete, harling and drunks.
But my mother, father and brother
are deserving. They are also dreamers
and dealers in words.

A Secretary, Bookkeeper, Print Finisher
and Teacher. Typewriters and ribbons.
Credits and debits. Glue, spines, covers.
Chalk, dusters, blackboards.
Black and white. Day after day.

The place that you grew up in does not
define you, although it is a part of you.
Dreams can be stolen, spirits broken.
However, I have picked up my pen
to break free from the mould.

DESTITUTION WALL

northbound ♦ concrete and platforms ♦ gables, kirks and ceilings ♦ healing stones and Saints

walls and summits ♦ chips by the roadside ♦ tumbles of pebbles ♦ shorelines at the land's edge

ash and looms ♦ dark rock ♦ sandy places ♦ a last note falls to earth ♦ Orion ♦ sweet heather

NO MAN'S LAND

The long concrete platform

between Northbound

and Southbound.

Pink pigeons flutter

under a glass roof.

Argent rails

touch infinity.

A yellow warning line

drops off the edge.

Two trains arrive

in a shimmer of heat.

Faces press

against windows.

The whistle blows.

Engines pull away.

Sound and metal disappear.

Arrivals and departures

linger.

CORROUR

The sliver of time

not long after a train

pulls out of the station

clock paused

at the moment of departure

silver rails

catching light.

SAINT MARY'S CHAPEL, GRANDTULLY

Dad stands
under the barrel roof,
silver haloed, fine hair catching light
from the small gable window.

A lone figure
at the far end of an empty church.
He points to the Renaissance ceiling,
marvels at fruit swags, coiled creatures,
parading birds, arms of Atholl, Lennox, Stewart,
scrolls, saints, angels, the centrepiece death scene.

Opening the heavy door, I step into a soft day.
A memory of hidden treasures,
the presence of my father
in the half light.

FILLIAN

Fillian hitches up his cassock
and strides into the Dochart.
Cold swallows his feet,
peat froth sweeps around his legs.
Golden birch leaves swirl
to settle in dark pools,
or ride the rapids rush.

He seeks the healing stones
and they seek him.
He feels for the parts of the body,
forms of heart, leg, arm, eye,
senses powers within the chosen eight.
Arms twitch and tug
like divining rods.

Up they come into the light,
showering baptisms of water.
Birthed from the '*scourer of all evil*',
forces unleashed from Breadalbane burns
and high mountain realms.
River worn, river blessed,
Dalradian black, umber, pearl silver.

Curious villagers gather,
some join him to be immersed.
Emerging, they gasp, clear their eyes,
argent droplets gleam on white skin.
He rubs the polished pebbles
over bodies, to cure all ills.
Christ is embraced.

Now, Fillian's relics
rest in dust and shadows,
his quidrich, bernane, mayne.
On Christmas Eve, a fresh layer
of leaves, river wrack and reeds,
cradles the healing stones,
dormant in their bed of straw.

DESTITUTION WALL

The wall is a strong spine
curving upwards, forging
across the grassy summit.

Up here in the cloud mist
is a long way from the croft
and the potato beds where forks
harvest the rot of blight.

Now they dig up stones
which cannot be eaten,
yet every stone is a mouthful.

The Lael carves its watery path
through the glen into Loch Broom.
And they would rather be down there
catching silver-scaled salmon.

But the deal is done and the thin ribs
of women and children moving
around like ghosts, cannot be ignored.

Every stone lifted,
every section built,
is a family struggling
into an uncertain future.

THE IMPORTANCE OF POTATOES

When you are eating chips,
or enjoying the warmth
of your comfortable guest house,
remember that where you
place your feet on the Iona road,
families died by the roadside
for want of a potato.
And it's just a thought
to remember what you have
and enjoy it.

NOUSTS

I see them where the fields fall
to the shore in tumbles of pebbles.
A row of grassy hollows, four yards by one,
indented, as though a giant's hand
has pressed into the earth.

Out in the timeless, sapphire Sound,
between pale Iona sands
and the pink granite of Kintra,
five boats drag sparkles of herring.
At dusk the tide carries them home.

Hands grab at coarse ropes
looped along the gunwales.
Each skiff is hauled to its noust.
Over the years keels shoogle and shift,
until the fit is snug as a glove.

I lie down in the groove,
long and bright like a herring,
long and straight like a wooden oar,
long and ribbed like a boat,
long and empty like a grave that waits.

GHOST BIRD

His whitewashed home clings to the land's edge,
like a polished whelk that brunts
the surge and slam of storm tides.
He scans long shorelines for precious wood,
gathers driftlings by the armful.
Boots crunch pebbles and dry dulse strands.
Above, black-backs soar empty margins.

Back at the house, an orange knot glows
in the blackened firebox. Flour, soda and salt
drift through sieve holes, buttermilk pools
in a bright sun that fills the china bowl.
Soon, dough puffs and browns, griddle hot.
He quarters a fresh baked farl, spreads butter,
lets the moist, creamy taste fill his mouth.

After tea, he sweeps the table
with a gull wing gleaned from the Corrán.
Fine flour dust spills into cupped hands.
He imagines a one-winged ghost bird
circling the island. And, over a lifetime,
he will take his knife, again and again,
to cut the cross on hot round bread.

THE PHILOSOPHY OF EGGS

Every morning Sinclair of Westray
placed two eggs and tea in the kettle.
He raked the ashes, set a match
to driftwood nested in the firebox.
Orange flames flickered,
chasing shadows across the room.

Pulling his jacket around broad shoulders,
he strode down the path into dawn light,
a thin line prising sky from sea.
Boots silvered with frost dust.

In the byre, flagstone floored,
fussing hens pecked at grain.
Sinclair pronged forkfuls of hay.
Lift, arc, shake, pale summer gold
shed itself through dank air,
collecting in corners and rafters.

Sweet machair straw mingled
with the sweet scent of cows
that nudged and jostled at the trough.
Outside, winter paralysed the land,
gathering ice lace around shorelines,
turning tussocks and webs to glass.

His breath steamed in the chill porch.
He hung up his old jacket,
warmed his hands at the stove.
Eggs rattled inside the kettle.
The spout beak whistled and sang.

Sinclair spooned his eggs on to the plate,
tap tapped his knife to crack the shells.
Lifting off brown stained tops,
he scooped out a bright sun in a white sky,
shiny buttercups, the colours of the gannet.

And the yolk spilling yellow at his Midas touch,
is a reminder of the other kind of yoke.
And the trust that he had in the small gleams
of treasure that the island offered,
lifted him out of the sweat and struggle.

Sinclair was a clever man you know. His eggs
were always the best, slow cooked, just perfect.

INVASION

Ropes have minds of their own.
They migrate to one another,
corkscrew across salty seas,
multi-coloured DNA spirals
congregate in bundles.

Some stranded on beaches,
brilliant Bluefire jellyfish,
long tentacles trailing.
Some, washed up swirls,
mini-galaxies
draped over black rocks.
Some, net-intact,
vibrant orange, fisherman yellow,
concertina diamond jersey patterns.
Some brittle with age, sun-baked,
degraded, weathered, weakened,
at a touch breaking into powdery filaments.

Assorted lengths float around
deep sea funnels and eddies,
hang around in crisscross rope shoals.
Swirling, shifting slowly,
catching penetrating light rays.
Natural hemp, woven, spliced, pleated, knotted,
rough ends frayed like lions tails.
Nylon, chemical blue, orange, yellow,
white, polished, ends melted.

Lost overboard from moorings, nets, rigging lines,
drifting for days and decades.
Thin, thick, twisted cords, curled, snake-entwined,
hitches, stopper knots, plaited.

Where do they all go in the end? To rope heaven?
To a giant universal rope brain with rope synapses
pulsing out messages like an international homing beacon?
Universal assembly harvested from ice scattered northern seas
and warm southern waters.

Modern art flotsam birthed from tankers, P and O's,
Feluccas, Hebridean yachts, local fishers,
Dover to Calais Norfolk line, Mediterranean cruisers,
shiny red funnelled Cal Macs, Chinese sampans.

Big tangles washed up on beaches all over the world.
Where eyes cast over them, ghost ships cast off.

AGA

A tangle of driftwood crackles
and argues in the firebox,
demanding a basketful of logs.

Yeast froths in a jug by the stove,
ready to be mixed with flour, salt, water.
The fat, silver kettle spits and hisses.

This Aga sailed across the sound
on the back of lashed together rowing boats,
fishes and loaves, loaves and fishes.

Silky dough is divided into two plastic bowls,
covered with a damp tea towel,
left to rise, plump, soft, round, warm.

There is no church at Scoraig, years ago
a man read a book about a spurned lover
who burnt down a church, so he did too.

He scoops it out with roughened hands,
push, stretch, fold, rock, thud,
push, stretch, fold, knock it back, let it rise.

Last year a house went up in flames,
nothing left except the Aga, intact,
standing in wet ash, a solitary altar.

Bread is cut, butter spread, tea poured.
The glass lamp reveals fine white dust motes,
shafts reach across wooden floorboards.

It has to be worshipped, ash removed,
wood offered, green enamel polished,
fat chimney flue cleared of resin.

The house sweats and rises in the heat.
Walls and roof expand, oven warm, muffled,
bread soft, moon plump, star grain scattered.

Aga temple glows intensely,
pine incense mingles
with sifted flour smoke.

SONG OF THE WEAVER

The colour of the pink
is in the ragged robin.
Come sings the weaver
come and thread my loom.

The blueness of the sea
is in the Minch expanse.
Come sings the weaver
come and thread my loom.

The yellow of the iris
is in the marshy ditch.
Come sings the weaver
come and thread my loom.

The purple of the heather
is on Beinn Ghobhlach's slopes.
Come sings the weaver
come and thread my loom.

The brown of the skylark
is soaring in the sky.
Come sings the weaver
come and thread my loom.

The green of the rowan
is in the fresh new bud.
Come sings the weaver
come and thread my loom.

Come sings the weaver
come and thread my loom,
come sings the weaver
come and join my tune.

Tweed for a shepherd,
cloth for a king,
into this weaving
nature's threads I bring.

LOOM

Wool combed scaffolding,
lanolin scented,

holds empty highways
which await the shuttle's passing,

the laying down
of thread upon thread,

for the weaver to sit and summon
swirling vibrant tweed lengths.

She and the loom
are a dark rock
on a sandy beach.

She and the loom
are musicians
playing an intimate duet,

feet pedalling
back and forth,
back and forth.

STAR MAN

Orion Star man runs
across Druim nam Fuath horizon,
roving chill November skies.

Feet push off cold land,
stride over James's croft
to snow-capped An Teallach.

Celestial followers accompany,
sword glitters at your side.

Run Orion run
through a million years of history,
eternal warrior of mankind.

ZARAGOZA

An ancient Tarrasius stirs in a Scottish stone
awakening distant Saragasso memories.

Anguilla migrates to mate and die
in deep Gyre spawning grounds.
Mini-pearls drift in warm Gulf currents,
transparent larvae emerge.

Glass Eel masses gather
along West Coast shorelines.
Mercurial strands, pinhead eyed,
advance towards ancestral Coigach.

Bubbling streams branch upwards,
divide, decrease, trickle, weave
around dark peat sedges.
Elver knots unravel.

The procession transforms,
sea silver to freshwater brown.
Catadromous carnivores slither
through decaying bracken arches.

Desolate moors, moon muted,
sketch enigmas of movement.
Living drill shafts, big sea-eyed,
silver rippled, bore down fast burns.

This soft place of mirror lochans
belongs to no one and everyone.
Life begins here and ends here,
oceans and clouds are born here.

Those who migrate
are compelled to return.

SNOW BRIDE

Silver crafted daisies,
six petalled, icy white,
fall at my feet.
Hexagonal symmetry,
perfect mathematics,
cold winter blossom.

Bridal glitter drifts
in looking-glass puddles,
confetti framed.
A veiled face looks up.
Enigma of a hundred
childhood thoughts.

A bride without a groom,
no cloying cake or relatives.
Better this way
than a little girl's make-believe,
happily ever after acted out
with blue-eyed dollies.

I walk the wild moor,
catching snow stars
that melt on warm hands.
Embroidered
from head to toe
in constellation filigree.

OTTER

A chocolate brown otter
stitches along the shore line

      in and out
          in and out.

A sleek underwater needle
piercing creamy satin loch hems.

Silver rings
radiate into polished water

echoing movement.

BLUE TIT

sips
icicle tips

under the eaves

light
catches
pale jasmine

soft blue

silver droplets
fall

in slow motion.

SOLOIST

Midnight blackbird
sings his heart out
on my rooftop.

A solitary
feathered
weather vane,

fluting
across the peninsula
to compass point
horizons.

A last pure note
falls
to earth.

Am feasgar a'ciaradh.
The evening growing dusky.

AUTUMN LADIES

Golden ballerina birches
billow and flounce

yellow ribbons criss-cross
silk silver waists

as they dance their way
into November.

THE WRITER

You always know when a poet

has been writing in bed,

blue-black ink streaks

trailing like comets

across white sheets.

ORIENTAL SNOW

A luxuriant orchid carpet,
Monet purple patterned,
laps my feet with dazzling silk.

Wind whips up sea meadows,
stirs billowing cotton grass,
wraps me in a summer snowstorm.

I head up to the high gate,
dance through shaking heather bells,
amethyst mottled, honey sweet.

Skip over wide mouthed sundews
and asphodel candles.
I am a machair flower girl.

Acrobatic dragonflies, gold-winged,
embroider yellow smoke trails
across vibrant moors.

HONEY AND STONE

bees, rifflers, lilies ♦ lands afar ♦ rock platforms and chasms ♦ pomegranate seeds

Olympians and ammonites ♦ boules in a limestone tunnel ♦ last spoonful of sweetness

HONEY AND STONE

The honey man
sets out his jars

of sweet dark amber,
gold lid capped.

He is a man of magic,
slim and dandy

in his silver buttoned
waistcoat and black felt hat.

Thick curls frame brown eyes
that dance like bees.

♦   ♦   ♦   ♦

The stonemason
sits next to him.

A solid, moon faced man,
hair stiff with dust.

He lays out chisels,
hammers, rifflers.

Strong hands carve green schist,
a delicate lily emerges.

Skin sparkles with minerals,
he is a colossal living stone.

*Midday, the square is empty
Silver glitters on cobbles.*

AMMONITE

A sharp stone impaled
in the bank by the path

is like a discus thrown
by an Olympian god.

With care I pull it out
and dust off crinkled edges.

It is remarkable to be standing
at the summit of Mont Saint Martin

holding a sea creature
that last saw light millions of years ago.

Here in my hand,
a cretaceous ammonite testimony.

ROTTEN PIGS AND WHEAT SEED

Pyanespsion, festival of Demeter and Persephone.

Anodos, first day, return of the maiden.

We wander uphill to Thesmophoria camp,
on the high rock platform of Pnyx.
I descend into the shadowed Megara chasm
to retrieve a suckling pig carcass. A sacrifice
to Demeter and Persephone. Clapping scares
snakes. Bones twist, shine, putrid flesh
falls away. Pine cones, dough serpents,
phalloi, are cast into the ravine.

Nesteia, second day of fasting, silence.

Silence until sunset. We eat only
fruit seeds; fresh, moist, crimson.
Foetid pig's flesh mixed with wheat
is placed on the big altar,
an ear of corn is shown.
A pomegranate sun descends
to earth. Sweet-cakes, formed
as female genitalia, are shared.

Kalligeneia, third day, goddess of beautiful birth.

We sing fertility songs, take a portion
of pig's flesh and seeds to bury in fertile fields,
a blessing for Demeter. At night torches blaze,
commemoration of her search for Persephone
in the underworld. We drink wine,
eat honey, figs, olives, sesame seeds,
make obscene jokes about our husbands.
The men will plant barley and winter wheat.

I pray that our gifts have been well received.

LA ROCHETTE TUNNEL

Blasted through in nineteen ten,
toppling medieval château ruins.
The village contours a limestone crest.
Heat bounces off tarmac.

Old men carrying chairs disappear
through the stone arch to play boules.
Balls click, click. Cigarette smoke wafts.
Earthy brick drips dampness and lime.

"Voiture, voiture, voiture!"
A Citroen winds around the road,
passes through in seconds,
pinning shadows to the wall.

At dusk the men gather
to sit by the war memorial.
Nineteen fourteen to eighteen;
Francois, Henri, Antoine, Marius.

Women in aprons bring cold beers,
unfold chairs, knit, chatter, gossip.
Tongues and needles click.
Haze blurs the tableau.

Children on bikes and scooters
swarm the cool, dark cavern.
Squeals echo, air reverberates.
Cicadas dissonance counterpoint.

LA DERNIÈRE CUILLÈRE

Resurrection
of raspberries and sugar.

Maman stands in her apron
and stirs the big silver jam pan.

Maman takes the wooden spoon
and pushes back wrinkles of crimson.

Maman lifts it to her lips
and tastes summer sweetness.

Isabelle takes a teaspoon
and scrapes it around the jar.

*"C'est la confiture de ma mère,
elle est décédée il y a quatre mois."*